NOUNS SAY "WHAT'S THAT?"

by Michael Dahl

illustrated by Lauren Lowen

PICTURE WINDOW BOOKS
a capstone imprint

Nouns give names to the world around us.

bus

We can name a person . . .

a place . . .

or a thing. Like that thing over there. That's a bus.

museum

entrance

statue

POINTING IS RUDE!

visitor

visitor

dog

dad

girl

boy

9

Names of particular people, places, and groups are called proper nouns. They always begin with a capital letter. All other nouns are called common nouns.

The world is full of proper nouns.

I see London! I see France!

When there are many nouns of the same type, a plural noun is used. Nouns often become plural by adding an "s" or "es" to their singular form.

student/students

"Singular" means one.
"Plural" means more than one.

bench/benches

One student, but a group of students.

Some nouns do not add an "s" or "es" to turn into plural nouns. They use a new word, a new noun.

children

child   child

person

We are

Daisy is a child. And Taj is a child. But together, Daisy and Taj are children.

Ms. Blossom is a person. And the museum guide is a person. But together . . .

THING

PERSON

19

Collective nouns are extra special. They describe groups—or collections—of people, places, and things.

flock

We call a group of athletes who play together a **team**.

We say a **flock** of birds and a **pack** of wolves.

A school of fish.

PERSON

THING

pack

TIMBER WOLF

team

24

25

A NUMBER OF NOTES ON NOUNS

Nouns are the names we give to people, places, and things.

Everyone you talk to or play with is a noun. (teacher, friend, cousin)

Everywhere you go is a noun. (park, mountain, kitchen)

Everything you see or smell or hear or taste or touch is a noun. (cloud, song, banana)

Some nouns are names we give to one special person, place, or thing.
We call them proper nouns. Proper nouns always begin with a capital letter.

Dr. Green   Statue of Liberty

Lake Michigan   my cat, Monster

Collective nouns name groups of people, places, and things.

flock (of birds)

pack (of wolves)

team (of football players)

band (of musicians)

Nouns can become plural by adding an "s" or "es," turning into new words, or by staying the same.

one reader, two readers

one lunch, two lunches

one mouse, two mice

one deer, two deer

ABOUT THE AUTHOR

Michael Dahl is the author of more than 200 books for children and has won the AEP Distinguished Achievement Award three times for his nonfiction. He is the author of the bestselling *Bedtime for Batman* and *You're a Star, Wonder Woman!* picture books. He has written dozens of books of jokes, riddles, and puns. He likes to play with words. In grade school, he read the dictionary for fun. Really. Michael is proud to say that he has always been a noun. A PROPER noun, at that.

ABOUT THE ILLUSTRATOR

Since graduating from the Illustration Department at the Rhode Island School of Design (RISD), **Lauren Lowen** has been creating art for a variety of projects, including publishing, ad campaigns, and products ranging from greeting cards and stickers to activity books and kids' luggage. She taught illustration at both Montserrat College of Art and RISD before becoming an instructor at Watkins College of Art in Nashville, Tennessee, where she currently lives with her husband and son. Some of her favorite things include sushi, chocolate milk, and Star Trek.

GLOSSARY

collective noun—a word that names a group of things

irregular noun—a word that doesn't form its plural by adding "s" or "es"

noun—a word that names a person, place, or thing

particular—one single thing chosen from many in a group

plural—more than one

proper noun—a word that names a special person, place, or thing

singular—just one

THINK ABOUT IT

1. What makes a proper noun different from a common noun?

2. Why are the words "tooth," "foot," and "deer" called irregular nouns?

3. Is "team" a collective noun? Why or why not?

READ MORE

Cleary, Brian P. *Feet and Puppies, Thieves and Guppies: What Are Irregular Plurals? Words Are CATegorical.* Minneapolis: Millbrook Press, 2011.

Heinrichs, Ann, and Danielle Jacklin. *Nouns.* Language Rules. New York: AV2 by Weigl, 2018.

Rosenthal, Betsy R. *An Ambush of Tigers: A Wild Gathering of Collective Nouns.* Minneapolis: Millbrook Press, 2015.

INTERNET SITES

Enchanted Learning: Grammar: Noun
https://www.enchantedlearning.com/grammar/partsofspeech/nouns/index.shtml

Grammaropolis: The Nouns
https://www.grammaropolis.com/noun.php

Schoolhouse Rock: Nouns
https://vimeo.com/2335546

LOOK FOR ALL THE PARTS OF SPEECH TITLES

INDEX

Editor: Jill Kalz
Designer: Lori Bye
Production Specialist: Katy LaVigne
The illustrations in this book were created digitally.

Picture Window Books are published by Capstone
1710 Roe Crest Drive, North Mankato, Minnesota 56003
www.capstonepub.com

Library of Congress Cataloging-in-Publication Data is available on the Library of Congress website.
ISBN 978-1-5158-3869-2 (library binding)
ISBN 978-1-5158-4058-9 (paperback)
ISBN 978-1-5158-3874-6 (eBook PDF)
Summary: Tour groups, exhibits, paintings, sculptures . . . The museum is teeming with common and proper nouns, everywhere you look! Person, Place, and Thing make sure readers not only discover factual grammar basics inside, but also lots of fun, laughter, and adventure.

All internet sites appearing in back matter were available and accurate when this book was sent to press.

Printed and bound in China.
001654